# Evening Plays

Books by Richard Maxwell

*Plays, 1996–2000: Richard Maxwell*
*Theater for Beginners*
*The Theater Years*

Richard Maxwell

Evening Plays

Theatre Communications Group  /  New York  /  2020

*Evening Plays* is published by Theatre Communications Group, Inc.,
520 Eighth Avenue, 24th Floor, New York, NY 10018-4156

The publication of *Evening Plays* by Richard Maxwell, through TCG's Book Program, is made possible in part by the New York State Council on the Arts with the support of Governor Andrew Cuomo and the New York State Legislature.

TCG books are exclusively distributed to the book trade by Consortium Book Sales and Distribution.

Library of Congress Control Numbers:
2018057922 (print) / 2018060580 (ebook)
ISBN 978-1-55936-581-9 (trade paper)
ISBN 978-1-55936-896-4 (ebook)
A catalog record for this book is available from the Library of Congress.

Design: 40 Worth St.
Cover Photograph: Michael Schmelling

First Edition, May 2020

# Contents

# The Evening

# Prologue

*Cammisa (as Beatrice) enters. She reads to the audience:*

One summer night, when I was six years old, I was playing in the kitchen of my house where I grew up and a large Native American man walked right in the back door of our house. He got caught in a thunderstorm and was very drunk. He entered in silence. I didn't dare move but I could see the man was oblivious to me, picking at leftovers on the counter. I went upstairs. "Papa, there's a stranger in the house." My mom and dad came downstairs and my dad fixed a plate for the hungry man who sobered up while he ate at our table and then my dad drove him home.

In what would be my dad's last days, I read that atoms are 99.9% empty space. I wondered, what is that one-tenth of one percent? And, is there no form because we're not here?

I kept trying to write while my dad was dying. As I wrote, I felt more and more like I was the one being written. Actually, the sensation was one of being unwritten, and without form.

He was betrayed by his body. Even in his ruinous state, the gap between life and death seemed an impossible chasm to get over.

I kept repeating, Another minute that passes is another minute with him in this world.

Amazing how much beginning there is in the end—training, meditating, dieting, revising, mowing...clinging to vain hope that the pain is caused by something—anything else. He tried to get better.

Journal of last days:

1:25 a.m. 10 mg of hydrocodone.

Restless nights. Sleeping most of the days. Family taking shifts: Bedtime to 3 a.m., 3 a.m. to waking up.

HE: "I don't even know where I am."

ME: You're at home. Do you know who I am?

"Richard?"

(I smile. We're holding hands.)

Do you want to get up?

He says, "Ok."

The bed they brought in is too small—he's always sliding down. Scootch him up. We're standing up, I realize he's stuck—catheter hose taut across the bed. I can't undo the damn velcro strap.

"Ok can you take a step to your left?"

He doesn't step.

"Can you step with me?"

(I'm holding him here, chest to chest.)

He takes a step and his legs start shaking. I set him down a little further up the bed.

Later, he sits up again. I go sit next to him at the foot of the bed rubbing his back.

Do you want a sip of water?

He says, "How does that work?"

He has a sippy cup. I go through my own parental reflexes.

I say, "Hey. It's very late."

"Is it?"

"Everyone is asleep. You should try to get some sleep."

I pick him up under his bony arms. His claw hands drop the pill.

Bizarre talk coming from both of us. Every decision I make I try to disguise as not pertaining to his performance—I am trying to normalize it all.

There were three major bird events during those last couple months:

In August, there was a murder of crows in the trees by the yard, and the roosting of hundreds of birds made it seem like you were in the face of an unseen and breathing cloud.

Then, in September, starlings amassed over by Peggy's house.

And eagles seemed to accumulate and soar, occasionally dousing the sun for a split second.

And ghostly tricks played out in the corners; phenomenal events that transcended time, and speech, and atmosphere.

I won't let him go. I can't.

Take walks to regroup.

And in the night, I took my source book to the bonfire at the farm. I secretly watched my family disperse, then I threw it in the remains of the fire and it burned up no problem.

The day he died:

It was a warm day, especially for Minnesota, sun streaming into the bedroom.

"What's going on? You ok?"

"No more questions!" he says.

"Ok, I want you to tell me what's going on, right now."

(I'm trying to get that wry sensibility happening between us again.)

He says, "I'm disoriented."

"Do you know where you are?" I ask.

"California?" he says.

My brother looks at me, smiles, and says, "It's warm enough to be California."

He sings songs with us on that day: "Goodnight Irene," "Jamaica Farewell," "You're the Only Star in My Blue Heaven."

He moves into a chair, his penultimate act. Then, incredibly, as his coup de grâce, he stands up on his own.

He took off, like out of sprinter blocks.

And after...the half-finished smoothie.

Rain came. It turned colder. The leaves fell.

Sprinklers, on a timer, came on around 5 a.m....

# Scene

# BAR

*A dive bar. A flat-screen TV behind the bar has football. There is a small stage in the stage-right corner with a backline setup: drums, amps, mikes on stands. Beatrice is behind the bar starting her shift. After a moment, Cosmo enters in coat with a pizza box.*

COSMO: Hey, Bee.

*He gives her a kiss, removes his coat and sits down. He opens his pizza box and takes a bite. Asi enters in parka.*

ASI: Hello, Cosmo.

COSMO: Asi! Congratulations my brother! You did it. YOU WON. You wore him down. You broke him. Give me a hug baby...You look good, you look good! YOU *ARE* GOOD. But he slipped, you saw that, right?

ASI: If you're telling me I look good then I know you suck.

COSMO *(laughing)*: No I mean it. Come on! I don't say shit like that without real feeling behind it.

ASI *(going over to Beatrice, gives her a kiss)*: I see you over there.

COSMO: You look like Freddy Krueger, but, hey, you won. You're amazing!

ASI *(back to Cosmo)*: You know I came down here because I thought you had something for me.

COSMO: ALL BUSINESS, HUH? Yeah, I know. I just hope I'm worthy of you. *(slaps him on the back. Asi winces)* You know I was watching you and thinking, this guy, he is at home, I LOVE WATCHING HIM—I feel like I'm in the hands of a master. It was a treat, it was a real treat to watch you fight, baby.

ASI: Eighteen years doing this.

COSMO: Yes, and *that experience*, SHOWED. And you get better and better.

ASI: Keep it alive.

COSMO: Peco says he can get you a fight with none other than KID HANSEN.

ASI: You mean OLD KID HAS-BEEN? I don't want to fight with JERRY, I want *new challenges*. I want to fight Benny.

COSMO: Hoh-no! Don't push your luck.

ASI: Do what I say.

*Pause.*

What are you drinking?

COSMO: Huh? This is water! What are you drinking? You want a beer? *(to Beatrice)* Get him a beer.

ASI: So what else do you got. I want to keep fighting.

COSMO: Ok—here's the plan. I talked to Jackie...we think you're ready for retirement. You know, you got to recover, so, we take this time to reconsider our options. I know you're tired. But, think of retirement as *marketing strategy.*

*Beatrice brings Asi's beer to the table.*

Asi: I'm not tired. Anyways, I can't retire. I got bills to pay. Speaking of which. *(to Beatrice)* Come here, baby.

*Asi gets Beatrice on his lap.*

Cosmo: You got to get through thinking these *dark-ass* thoughts.

Asi: Don't worry about me. Look at this little girl.

Cosmo: She's not that little.

Asi: No, she is that little. *(to Beatrice)* You saw that fight, baby? You know I won that for you.

Beatrice: I heard something. Been pretty busy.

Asi: Yeah, I fight for you. If you want money, I got it.

*Beatrice gets up, returns to bar.*

Beatrice: Five thousand dollars?

Asi: Yeah what would you do for that?

Beatrice: Nothing like that.

Asi *(standing up)*: Come on! Why not. Five thousand? I'll give it to you if you— *(mouthing something to her)*

BEATRICE *(laughing)*: No!

*Asi smiles.*

Why don't you call me when you get out from under his thumb.

ASI: What? I'm not under—...you got jokes... *(looking at Cosmo)* Him? He works for me.

BEATRICE: That's not what he says.

ASI: Oh yeah? *(still on Cosmo)* Tell me what he says.

COSMO *(meeting his stare)*: You know what? Give me a small beer.

ASI: This meeting is over.

*Asi puts on his coat and heads for the door. Cosmo rises to intercept.*

COSMO: What! Wait a second! You're pretty high-handed, like that.

ASI: They told me you quit and I knew I couldn't believe it!

COSMO: All right! *(to Beatrice)* Forget it.

ASI: For all I know, you've been drinking all along!

*Pause.*

COSMO: Then go.

*Pause. Asi stays.*

You know...You're an angry dude.

Asɪ: It's good for the cage.

Cosмo: Save it for the cage!

Asɪ: Get me that fight!

Cosмo: I'm working on it. Come on. Sit down.

*Cosmo gets his beer, raises it to Asi as an invitation, then sits down. Asi doesn't move.*

Listen, as long as that anger stays with you, you'll be a magnet for trouble. You know what you need? You need a girlfriend. You should get with a dancer. I'm with a dancer right now. If you've never been with a dancer then you don't know what you're missing. She takes off her clothes without thinking about what it means to viewing eyes, and the subtle ways she manipulates my flesh, never knew how *in tune* a person could be. You need to get laid.

Asɪ *(still standing, with eyes locked on Beatrice behind the bar)*: I'm working on it!

Cosмo: You need to get out.

Asɪ: I'm here, aren't I?

Cosмo: Yeah, you need to *see people*.

Asɪ: I see just fine.

Cosмo *(gets up, pulling out his phone)*: Maybe you should get high. *(showing his phone to Asi)* Look at that? Isn't it beautiful?

Asɪ: What is that?

COSMO: It's a bud. —Relax! I'm not buying it, I'm selling it. Yeah so listen! What was I saying?

ASI: You are gonna get me that big fight.

COSMO: I would, but you are not strong enough and you're not smart enough. And you're not good looking, at all. Period. *(laughs, looking for an audience. Asi steps behind him putting him in a double-ear hold)* ...Yeah, YEAH! That's it. Get pissed! Get mean! You gonna need that, YE-AH...You still feel depressed you fucking— *(Cosmo howls in pain)* FUCKING STOP YOU PIG.

*Asi releases Cosmo.*

That smarts!...See that? Got you goin, didn't I? That's the eye of the tiger, right there.

*Pause.*

I'm using you, you're using me. We both get what we need. We're in the same room. Those are the facts.

ASI: Like islands.

COSMO: Yeah, like islands. I'm happy. Are you happy?

ASI: No. I'm not fucken happy.

COSMO: You won! What do you want?

*Pause. Cosmo gets up and stands by the bar.*

I wanna get out of town. I wanna go where people aren't so down all the time. All the bad moods get me down and rub off on me.

I want to go to an island. Doesn't that sound good? Beautiful. Natural resources. Hard to get to, I'll go there live in peace, and hopefully it won't get discovered by anyone. I'll live there, defenseless, a little bored at times. Got to get to an island.

BEATRICE *(walking over to Asi)*: I want to talk to you.

ASI: What. I didn't come down here to see you. He called me.

BEATRICE: I want to go to Istanbul.

ASI: What?

BEATRICE: I want to go to Istanbul.

ASI: What's in Istanbul?

COSMO: Hash.

ASI: Why the fuck would you be going to Istanbul. What's in Istanbul.

COSMO: Hash.

ASI: Shut up. Istanbul? Why?

BEATRICE: Because it's not here. I'm hoping it's the *opposite* of here.

ASI: What the fuck. What for.

BEATRICE: For a trip. For fun.

ASI: Well I can't go I'm busy.

BEATRICE *(laughing)*: I don't want to go with you. I want to go by myself.

ASI: You can't do that.

BEATRICE: Why not?

ASI: You have a job.

BEATRICE: You don't know my job.

ASI: All right fine. But what's this about you wanting to go to Istanbul?

BEATRICE: You know. Look. A lot of people have died on me, lately, and. Yeah. I mean fuck. What are you supposed to do when you miss people? I didn't expect this. So, it's a trip, you know, and I've been saving up for it. I finally got enough money to go. So.

*Cosmo goes back to his chair, sits.*

ASI: But listen. I don't want you to go.

BEATRICE: Why not.

ASI: Cos I'm worried about you. And ah.

BEATRICE: What.

ASI: I don't know. I just. I don't want to see you spend your money that way.

BEATRICE: Well, I've already been kicked out of where I was and I didn't have a place to stay and.

Asi: Then stay with me.

Beatrice: I'm not moving back in with you. It's just more of the same. I need to change camp.

Asi: Please don't go. It's not safe! Come on.

Beatrice: No your home is not safe. Anyway, think about it, I'm working.

Asi: What the fuck...I just think about what if you don't come back? If you need money, I can get it to you, but you're not goin to Istanbul!!

Beatrice: I want to get out of here I just wanna fuckin—I don't want to have anything to do with this place. I don't want to be associated with all this. I'm tired of it.

Asi: Yeah, well you got to. That's the sad part. Wherever you go you gonna need people. I'm sorry about the family stuff. But you move on. You're needed here.

Beatrice: You do move on. And I believe being alone is good for me. I can't change my plans. I'm sorry. I got to get out of here and I've waited too long for this. I'm not giving this up.

Asi: Well you are not going. You are staying.

Beatrice: I am going. I feel bad, but that's that.

Asi: YOU'RE NOT FUCKING GOIN!

Beatrice: I'm sorry!

Asi: I can't believe it...So it's like that? Unreal. *(to Cosmo)* See what I'm talking about? There's no reason for her going. *(to Beatrice)* Is there something you are not telling me? What is it? I don't know what you are.

Beatrice: It's sad, that's done, and in the past. I'm going forward. I leave tomorrow.

Cosmo: I think you should go.

*Pause.*

She should go, no?

*Pause.*

Asi *(measured, at Cosmo)*: This is not your business.

Cosmo: I want her to go where she wants to go and then she'll come back. This isn't prison. That reminds me. Buddy of mine once sent a joint to somebody in prison. And puts a return address on there. What a dumbass.

Asi: You're staying with me.

Beatrice: Don't embarrass yourself.

Cosmo: She can go if she wants to go. *(getting up and in between them, gently pushing Asi backward)* Can we please just have a good time. Listen—

Asi *(to Beatrice)*: *That's very fucked up that you're doing that.* You're just a kid!

Cosmo: She can do some things.

*Pause.*

Asi *(to Cosmo)*: Who are you to say anything?

*Pause.*

Cosmo: I speak my heart.

*Asi and Cosmo square off.*

*Cosmo pulls out a small zippered kit, hands it to Asi.*

Here, take your steroids, Asi.

*Asi considers for a moment, then takes the kit, and starts to prep the syringe. He drains the bottle with the needle, then pulls his training pants down.*

Asi *(holding the full syringe)*: I don't get it. I just don't get it. It's not supposed to play out like this.

*Pause.*

How am I supposed to prepare for the thing that isn't gonna happen?

*A band enters stage left, numbering three, with coats on and gig-bags slung on shoulders. Asi, Cosmo and Beatrice note them as they pass. Asi stabs the needle into his thigh, pulls up his pants and tosses the kit on the table.*

I don't accept it. I refuse to accept. I'm a fighter that's what I do. *(to Beatrice)* What does victory mean, anything to you?

*Pause.*

In my life. If I see something I like, I grab it.

*Pause.*

That's just how it is. Do you see that?

*Pause.*

And. If I say I love you, it means I love you.

*Pause.*

I'm not saying I love you. But if I did.

*Pause.*

But I think I do love you.

*Pause.*

I really do think that sometimes.

*Pause.*

I feel that. And. What do you feel baby?

*Pause.*

It seems we've been through a LOT.

Cosmo *(standing up)*: I don't understand, why can't we just have *fun*? Come on. Get a drink. Let me get you a drink. Relax. You know?...Come on! Please? Can we have fun? I don't get it. *(the band begins to play)* You know. It's— Why can't you just—celebrate a little bit? We don't have to celebrate something from now, we could celebrate something else, like, from a year ago...anything...jeeziz, let's have some fun for a change. I love this song. *(starts dancing)* Come on. *Just have fun for a while!!*...It's fun.

*Song: "Uncomplicated."*

Band:

Do you remember?
Playin rough and rowdy
On the merry-go-round
With the older kids
Feeling strong, runnin hard, all golden tan
Uncomplicated

Hair like a banshee
A rope for a belt
Barefoot in blue jeans, with the cuffs rolled up
Kick-the-can, statue tag, as the sun set
Uncomplicated

*At Cosmo's urging, Beatrice and Asi dance together in front of the bar, while Cosmo bops by the band. Beatrice whispers something to Asi, Asi stops dancing, goes to Cosmo and pushes him into a wall, giving him a "wake-up" smack.*

Asi *(over the music)*: Did you give her money for the trip??

Cosmo: Yeah, a little.

Asi: I told you that is VERY FUCKED UP. You deal with me you don't deal with her!

*Asi crosses back to Beatrice.*

What did you do for *him* that he gives you money?!

*Asi moves to the table, staring at Cosmo, who is standing at the back wall. Cosmo, unbothered, picks up his pizza box, flips it open and digs in.*

Cosmo *(chewing)*: Did you ever notice how trouble just follows you around? People argue with you, and people get in your face, what is that? At a certain point, you have to ask yourself, "Maybe it's me?"

*Pause.*

Asi: Look at you. You used to be in such *great shape*. Now, you get high and eat pizza.

*Cosmo smiles, toothily.*

Cosmo: Come on, you two were dancing so nice. Dance together.

*Cosmo puts down the pizza box and brings Beatrice to Asi. Cosmo watches them slow dance, then dances pressing himself into Beatrice, unbeknownst to Asi. They dance as three for a moment.*

Asi *(comprehending)*: What the fuck are you doing? What's going on?

*Cosmo laughs. Asi stalks, Cosmo retreats. Beatrice, caught in the middle, tries to keep them apart.*

Cosmo: Just having fun! It's a joke!

Asi: Do you see what I am?

Cosmo: I do. Crazy.

Asi: It's not crazy. Because you know what I'm talkin about. And I'm here for BUSINESS. You know what I'm saying. Yeah, you do. Most guys like me fight to submission. *(Asi pushes Cosmo)* I fight to *the death.*

Cosmo: I need someone to show me how to fight to the death. Do you think you could show me how to fight to the death?

*Asi steps on top of the table.*

Asi: Perhaps I will. I fight with my hands and I can kill with them—look at my hands. *(presenting the back of his hands to Cosmo)* I got calcium deposits in my knuckles.

Cosmo: Do you think you can show me how to fight to *the death*?

*Asi plunges down on top of Cosmo and they wrestle.*

Beatrice: Stop. Stop it!

*The men grapple to the floor with Beatrice sandwiched between them. Cosmo proceeds to pin Asi's shoulders with his knees and punches him repeatedly, while Beatrice kicks helplessly.*

Asi: Ahhhggghh!!

*End of "Uncomplicated."*

Cosmo: That's a lot of testosterone right there!...I'm sorry, I took advantage. You just fought yesterday, that's why.

*Asi wrests loose, backs off and straightens himself.*

Asi: All right. All right! *(to Beatrice)* COME ON!! WE'RE LEAVING!

Beatrice: We're not leaving.

Asi: Get your things.

Beatrice: What things? I'm working.

*Pause. A détente as they resume their former positions at the table and behind the bar.*

Cosmo *(to Beatrice, pointing out placements)*: Beer, beer, beer; jello, jello.

*Song: "Sun," an instrumental.*

*Beatrice brings the men beers and jello shots.*

*Pause.*

I like this place, I'm not going to lie. Can't really think of any better place to be. Where can you go when you want to get away? The city doesn't let you run away to just anywhere so go where you need to be when you just want to hang out...

*Pause. He drinks.*

There's something to be said for a person who needs to be

protected. Look at us. Who doesn't want to be comforted. I'm talking to you but I might as well be talking to...the royal "you." You've wronged on some score and so all that's left for you is to complain about the others...and you want protection, comfort.

*Pause. He drinks.*

This is the only place you can go. The only fun is booze places like this. So be thankful.

*Pause. He drinks.*

I remember illegal parties and busted-out warehouses and pot-enclaves and free-scenes and memory. I remember oases of dark shaded green for adults deemed responsible enough to be *left alone*...I want some coke. Can I get some coke?...Can't get it?

*Pause. Cosmo is drinking. Asi crosses to bar and snatches Beatrice's phone out of her hands.*

BEATRICE *(coming around the bar)*: Give me my phone. Hey!

ASI: Who are you texting!

*Asi takes her picture.*

Let me see you. Smile.

BEATRICE: Stop it!

*Beatrice tries for the phone behind Asi's back, backs up and returns behind the bar.*

*End of "Sun."*

*Song: "Moon."*

BAND:

I am an "Asi"
I cling to the poesy
A universe of me
I speak poetry

Do not exile me
Just give me poetry
Moon moon and moon
The town and the moon

One more time
Please make it last
The town and the moon

ASI *(sits on a stool, holding Beatrice's phone)*: I can't let you go. You're in everything. You're in the walls. You're everywhere. I really need you. You know that, right? You don't know now, but you will. What is it? Everything that I could ever possibly want, you give me. You know. All my desires. You meet me step for step. You anticipate what I need, where I am. Why am I here, like this? It's like you are a reflection of myself that pleases me. What am I that this is possible? I hope I'm not flattering myself to say that I am worthy of your company. My guide.

*Pause. Cosmo drains his drink and sidles up to the bar. He pulls out a big bag of weed and sets it in front of Beatrice.*

COSMO: You want to go, he doesn't want you to go. But if it were up to me, I would return. Converge backwards tonight. You know? I have the means *(pats the bag)* and I...c'mon... *(Beatrice won't look at him)* ...Are you working?

*He fans out a wad of bills, then showers the bills over her.*

*End of "Moon."*

Hello? Give me a beer?

*Beatrice gets him a beer.*

*Pause. Cosmo returns to his table, drinks, but doesn't sit.*

*Song: "Hill."*

BAND:

If I admit all the things to you
Like, how separate and afraid I feel
Like thin glass smashed inside my chest

How dread culls the skeleton
Would I come undone?
You're on your phone I'm on my phone there's no *"phone for you!"*
Would I come undone?

As we walk
Up the rise together
As they meet
Our eyes
Can't get anywhere
Other than here

*Beatrice, downcast, is standing behind the bar. She picks up a 9 mm pistol, walks around to the front of the bar, points it at Asi's face.*

BEATRICE: Give me my phone.

*Asi hands back her phone. Cosmo turns and sees the gun and backs up.*

Asi: Where'd you get that?...Hey, quit fucking around.

Beatrice: I'm very unsure with this thing...I don't really know.

Asi: You don't play with that.

Beatrice: I don't really know. I DON'T REALLY KNOW!

Asi: Ok, ok! Stop! That's enough. What is this?

Beatrice: Never fired a gun before...

*Pause.*

Who should care?

Asi: I care.

Beatrice: No...Who *should* care? I don't fit in, I feel left out... Who cares. Words without. I am a prostitute slash bartender in one lonely corner of the universe. On that scale of things—who should care?

*Beatrice puts the gun to Asi's chest and backs him down into his chair. She then levels the gun at Cosmo and backs up to a stool in front of the bar, sits, placing the gun on the bar.*

*End of "Hill."*

*She puts her head in her hands.*

*Pause. Cosmo goes to the bar.*

Cosmo *(looks at Asi, then to Beatrice)*: Do you ever...Do you ever just wish there was a—place where you could be away from this, outside...the lines?

*Beatrice lifts her head.*

BEATRICE: Yes. I do.

Cosmo: I find that place when I get really, really high? But. Um. I want—I want you to be...alone...not for me...I want. Love but. I want love, but...I do want it. But...there's just no time. And, we could be together in some place in some way but that's not what I want. For you. You know? There's always love, I know, but. Without all these barriers and father time. You know? It's like there's no trust at all. It's like—no genuine hope at all. Like that. And with you it could be like that. I really want you to go.

*Song: "Stars."*

BAND:

Mmm-mm
Radio light take me tonite
You will be my morning star
I want to get lost in your songs
And find her tonite on the line

Hey old soul, you never get old
Get past the names of everything
Here on earth, it's how it goes
So turn this one out, on the dirt road

Pedal down
Faster than sound

I go too fast
To stay on the ground

Let me share something with you
It's been a dark summer
As you build up it comes apart
Pray for a break in these clouds

Spinning wheels
We're gonna fly
Cut the sky
Open the light
Mmm-mm

*Asi watches Cosmo.*

BEATRICE: Do you like me?

COSMO: I do.

BEATRICE: I don't feel worth much.

*End of "Stars."*

COSMO: Yes, I like you.

BEATRICE: I just yearn for so many who've come before us. And I want to see them. I find it a comfort to think that they're with us, out there, somewhere.

COSMO: Who are they? Family?

BEATRICE: The doctor said he's not gonna get better. And you think, What are you talking about? Who's going to be the guy on the road who stops when you stick out your thumb?

*Pause.*

I feel like we're the losers. We must be. Because we lost. You know? Are we the losers?

COSMO: No. I don't think so.

BEATRICE: We are though. We're the ones left.

*Song: "Valley," an instrumental.*

COSMO: We're outcasts, maybe. We're undesirables...But. We can't be "losers" as long as we have each other. At least we have each other.

BEATRICE: With us, it's always assumed there are persons behind us. But I think we're forgotten. I think we got left behind. It's like. The machine shuts off, knowing no one will ever have the time or care to look back at this. And I walk up to the lines that have been drawn and I shy away every time. Every time. I—dreams...I have these—suffocating dreams. Where the end really means, *the end*...It's like, I am caught between *two worlds* and the dreams keep me from getting out and into either one.

COSMO: Will you try getting out?

BEATRICE: Yes. Yes, I will.

*Pause.*

COSMO: Which way will you try?

BEATRICE: I don't know but I want...ever-changing.

COSMO: Ever-changing, yes...what.

BEATRICE: Ever-changing...camps.

COSMO: Camps, yes. I could see that. For you. Ever-changing camps. That would be a feat.

*Cosmo lunges for the gun. Beatrice snatches it first and her gun arm goes taut, aiming at Cosmo, then Asi, then back at Cosmo. Asi crouches at the table. Cosmo doesn't move.*

*End of "Valley."*

BEATRICE: What are you?

COSMO: Huh?

BEATRICE: What are you, tell me what you are. I said what I am so what are you?

*Pause.*

COSMO: Uh. People are pleasure to me. I also like to get high. I exist but I have given up. I am the reminder that you resign. That's all that you do, ultimately. You cannot win, and that is ok. Maybe you lose, but there is pleasure.

BEATRICE *(pointing the gun at Asi)*: And what are you?

*Pause.*

ASI *(straightening)*: I'm a fighter. I fight. I look out at the world. I recover to heal in time for the next battle. I will win and keep on winning.

BEATRICE: Who cares. We don't do bad things, only do understandable things. Fuck who we want, ingest what we want, do what we want. We, whatever.

*Asi moves to Beatrice until she stops him with the gun.*

Asi: Are you for real??

Beatrice: I don't know. Let's see. Is this real? *(puts the gun to Asi's forehead)* Feel that, motherfucker.

*Beatrice backs Asi up. Asi pushes a chair between them.*

Cosmo: Ok, enough gun play. Enough already.

*Beatrice cocks the gun.*

Asi: Don't shoot me...Are you crazy? What's going on? Talk to me here!

Cosmo: Don't.

Asi: You know what? Wait a second. Wait a second. What did I do?

*Beatrice shoots Asi. The sound of the shot presses into the room. Blood splatters.*

*Pause.*

*Asi puts his hand on his chest and it gets covered in blood. He looks at his hand, then at Beatrice.*

...Jeez, I don't know what to say. It seems like things are crumbling all around us...The police are going to come.

BEATRICE: They're not.

ASI: I'm gonna die.

BEATRICE: No you're not.

ASI: Then take me to the hospital.

BEATRICE: No.

*Pause.*

*(pointing gun at Cosmo)* What do you think?

*Cosmo looks at Asi. Then back to Beatrice.*

COSMO: You should try it.

*Beatrice fires the gun at Cosmo. More blood.*

You shot me. *(looking at the blood)* ...Why'd you do that?

*Pause.*

*Beatrice tosses gun on table. She goes to Cosmo. She unzips his jacket and finds the apparatus for making the blood effect attached inside. She pulls it out and puts it on the table. It is plastic tubes and copper wires, stained with blood. Asi opens his hoodie to find the same apparatus.*

*Pause.*

What's going on? Where are we?

*Pause.*

BEATRICE: We're not here.

*Pause.*

ASI: At least we have each other.

BEATRICE: What are you talking about?? We don't have each other. I'm *out*.

ASI: You're not out. You're here. You got nothing left if you leave.

*Beatrice looks for a way out behind the band.*

What are you doing? Why are you over there.

BEATRICE: I'm trying to get as far away from you as possible.

ASI: Why do you fuck things up like this?

*Beatrice crosses back to the bar, puts on her coat.*

BEATRICE: I just know this isn't enough!!

ASI *(to the band)*: What's a matter with you. Play, dammit! *(to Beatrice)* What's going on.

BEATRICE: I'm going someplace else. I—

*The band begins to play.*

ASI: Istanbul?

BEATRICE: Fuck Istanbul. I don't want to be...

ASI: You know what I mean. Who's gonna adore you? Like me.

BEATRICE: No one.

ASI: I want to keep fighting. I don't want to retire, I want to keep fighting. I want to—hey, let me go with you then.

BEATRICE: Stop it. You can't come with me.

ASI: Well then you go and I'll just be walking in the same direction.

BEATRICE: No.

ASI: You packed a suitcase.

*Song: "Ice."*

BAND:

You give too much shade
I want to stop this dreaming
I saw the dark

Take your covers off
I want to see your faces
And feel your hands

I can see her glowing
As she walks ahead
I like her glow

Many came before
She can change the weather
Now here she comes

BEATRICE: Days ago.

*Asi begins to pace.*

ASI: Need to pack my things. Don't forget anything. What will we need on this trip? Oxygen, washcloth, water, dramamine, heavy coat...you know, this is like a trip I wanted to take for years and we never could...I used to be great. It's true. I could hold you in my bicep. I trained every day. I was amazing. You get older. It's just something to get used to. But that's ok. I'll get it back. I always get it back.

BEATRICE: The things you say don't matter anymore. Do you see that?

ASI: Please! PLEASE. You're thinking of it all wrong. You *get* to do all this...We live in this garbagey void, of all the old tropes of standing still and forgotten dreams, it's a...masculine world coming from the container, with triangles and tired heroes. We traffic in made-up rough bars and broke-up chairs. We position ourselves in fitting geometry. We rehash family and letting go, and love. We do that mysteriously, yet familiarly. We do that and keep circling around... Circling around...*and it's great!*

*End of "Ice."*

BEATRICE: Bye.

COSMO: Bye.

*Beatrice turns to face the audience.*

BEATRICE: What right do I have to feel...free?

Asɪ: You're not free. You're with me.

Cosmo: She's going to leave now. Let her try.

Asɪ: *I don't want to retire. I want to keep fighting. Live to see one more fight...I don't want to retire. I want to keep fighting. Live to see one more fight...*

*Song: "Ghosts."*

Band:

We're joined tonite
By the ghosts of those
The ghosts of those
Concerned

Who do I sing to?
Now that you're gone
If you can't receive
And won't return

But where can I meet you?
I'll rise to that line

*Beatrice steps toward the audience and out of the bar. During the rest of the song, the bar comes apart and the stage is struck by stagehands. Asi and Cosmo strike themselves. The band is left for last, finishing the song with whatever is left for them. Meanwhile, Beatrice pulls the top of a white ghillie suit out of her bag and puts it on, covering her head with the hood and veil. Fog begins to roll in.*

I'll go where'er
That portal leads

Then we shall see
Each other

I feel your love
Extending past the lines
Up to and including the Isle of Skye

What do the ghosts need
You thought they could read
Our minds

But they can't
They need to see
To see it written down

Have you seen
All that one can see?
No you have not seen
All the beauty

Keep writing I love you
Keep writing I love you

Keep calling "I love you"
I love you
Keep calling "I love you"

*End of "Ghosts."*

# Scene

## RITUAL

*Silence. The bar is gone, revealing a large empty white room full of fog. Cammisa, alone on stage, assesses her new surroundings, then speaks to the audience.*

CAMMISA: In the distance, Cammisa finds snow-capped peaks. She climbs...She looks out at the landscape, a line she thinks she sees against the sky.

*Pause. The fog continues.*

Cammisa plunges down and walks at the bottom of oceans...She descends even further into the core of the earth.

*Pause.*

Cammisa walks until she comes to a river with a swift current.

*Pause.*

Cammisa finds the bottom of the other side and gets onshore and with the water lapping, turns around, clothes wet.

*Pause.*

The moon is out. She continues.

*Cammisa walks away, tracing the boundaries, finally disappearing into the fog.*

Samara

# Scene 1

*The Outpost. An active place. Wood interior. Daylight from the entrance. A supervisor is here. A messenger with a backpack stops him.*

MESSENGER: Sirrah, I need to get paid. With whom do I speak?

SUPERVISOR: Well just ask whoever is on duty.

*The messenger looks around. The supervisor moves paper around. The messenger comes to look on the supervisor.*

MESSENGER: *You're* on duty.

*The supervisor continues to busy himself. The messenger waits. The supervisor sighs, opens the drawer at his belly, looks in.*

SUPERVISOR: Uh. There's one problem...

*He shrugs at the messenger. The messenger shrugs back.*

Step back, please.

*The messenger does not move.*

You know, there's a whole big picture that you're not going to see. And I'm not going to trouble you with. But there is a sense, here, that favors are not automatic, you...you get to know people...and, as you get to know people here—here, here's seven dollars...

MESSENGER: Seven dollars is not what I'm owed.

SUPERVISOR: I don't know what to tell you.

MESSENGER: I did my job, sirrah. *Everything* asked of me—

SUPERVISOR: —No, wait.

*He pulls an old beat-up piece of paper out of his pocket.*

This one owes me money.

MESSENGER: What's this?

SUPERVISOR: More than you're owed. You can collect from him, if you can find him.

MESSENGER: No, take it back. I'm not collecting other people's debts. I want the money I'm owed.

SUPERVISOR: I don't know what to tell you.

*Pause.*

MESSENGER: Give me the seven dollars. I'm through with you and your lot.

*The messenger walks outside into the light. He walks back inside.*

Gimme the paper.

SUPERVISOR: Gimme seven dollars.

*The messenger gives him seven dollars. The supervisor counts it and gives him the paper. The messenger inspects the paper.*

MESSENGER: How far?

SUPERVISOR: Six days, if you're lucky.

*The messenger turns, exiting.*

Someone outside might help you, like a hired gun or something.

MESSENGER: I don't need a gun.

SUPERVISOR: One moment!

*The messenger stops.*

There is one thing.

MESSENGER: What is it?

SUPERVISOR: I can't find my knife. Know anything about that?

*Pause. The messenger turns around, watching the supervisor, and rolls up the sleeves of his shirt, revealing cut marks and scars on his forearms. He then hitches up the front of his shirt revealing a knife holstered in the waist of his pants. He smiles.*

MESSENGER: I don't know anything about your knife.

SUPERVISOR: Let me see something.

*The supervisor comes around and moves to grab the messenger's wrist. The messenger steps back.*

You took my knife. Give it back.

*The supervisor lunges for the messenger, who slips away, playfully evading the supervisor until the supervisor, breathless, captures him in his arms. The messenger draws the blade and stabs the back of the supervisor. The messenger lets the supervisor fold out and roll off.*

*He regards the dying man, turns, and exits the town. Before him is endless plain. Beyond that, valley and river. Beyond that, vast hills.*

## Scene 2

*The other side, before the rains. Sweltering heat. The manan and the drunk. The manan is behind the bar, the drunk is parked at one end, with two coins and heavy thoughts. The drunk has been looking at a map.*

DRUNK: All torn apart and missing parts. Just had to leave. Time to go on. Time to go.

MANAN:

DRUNK: We are deliberate proof that you can disappear, if you want to.

MANAN:

DRUNK: Do you see us there? See what I mean?

MANAN:

DRUNK: Me and you, we took ourselves off the map.

MANAN:

DRUNK: There are numerous possibilities for why we disappeared, ranging in scope from earth to the body to the mind to the spirit. But...

MANAN:

DRUNK: In the end, that's all history and words. We are here. Not there.

MANAN:

*The drunk tears up the map.*

DRUNK: Now, neither you, nor I.

MANAN:

DRUNK: And, still we have each other.

MANAN:

DRUNK: There's nothing wrong with saying it, and I never get tired of hearing it. Even when you're all alone and you know *no one* else will say it...But. Don't you still like to hear it?

MANAN: Hear what?

DRUNK: "I love you."

MANAN:

*Pause.*

DRUNK: Some day, I will ask you to marry me, and I know what you will say. You will say, "No," because you and I both know, there is no need for it. And I understand: Life is going to play out in the same way, right?...So. Pick a color.

MANAN:

*Pause.*

DRUNK: You thought it was going to be hard.

MANAN: No.

DRUNK: No!

MANAN:

DRUNK: It's not going to be hard.

MANAN: It's not going to be hard!

*Pause.*

DRUNK: When it cools off. After the rains. You and me will get together. I feel it coming back to me. You just stay the way you are. Don't change a thing. It'll come back, G.

# Scene 3

*The messenger rides and rides. Then he climbs and climbs. The journey takes its toll. He arrives at the bar, weather-beaten and out of breath.*

MANAN: Someone send you?

MESSENGER:

MANAN: You want something to drink?

*Pause.*

Eh—come over! This—

DRUNK: What the—?

MANAN: What's the deal? What is your name, sir? Oh! He stinks! What is your name?

MESSENGER:

*The messenger collapses. The manan and the drunk lay him out.*

# Scene 4

*The bar, the next morning.*

DRUNK: Is he dead?

MANAN: Wouldn't be the worst thing.

DRUNK: Who is it?

MANAN: I don't know.

DRUNK: Do you know, why him?...Here?

MANAN: Yeah, I have an idea.

DRUNK: Ok, what.

MANAN:

DRUNK: ...That is?

MANAN: I'm afraid if I say it, it will be true.

DRUNK:

MANAN: He's a kid!

*The drunk approaches the messenger. The messenger rises.*

MESSENGER: Who is Hilton?

MANAN: That's my father.

MESSENGER: Where is he?

*Pause.*

MANAN: He's dead.

MESSENGER: You know this?

MANAN: Yes sir.

*The messenger hands the manan the slip of paper.*

MESSENGER: I bought your father's debt. You owe me my wages. I've traveled eleven days.

# Scene 5

*The bar, late afternoon the next day. The manan and the messenger. The drunk is watching.*

MESSENGER: Where should I put my gear?

MANAN: Your gear. Um. Just there.

MESSENGER: Yeah.

MANAN: How long you planning to stay with us.

MESSENGER: Until I get paid.

MANAN:

MESSENGER: You understand that?

MANAN: It's late in the season is all. I wouldn't want you to get stuck out here.

*Pause.*

MESSENGER: Don't worry about me.

*Pause. The messenger stares at the manan for a time.*

Can I ask you something? Please don't take offense.

MANAN: What is it.

MESSENGER: Nah, I really shouldn't.

MANAN: What.

MESSENGER: What...what are you?

*Pause.*

MANAN: What am I what?

MESSENGER: All right...that's all right. I won't ask. Pardon me.

*The drunk turns away.*

What is this place you have here? An inn?

MANAN: I suppose.

MESSENGER: It's an inn. You take boarders. Fine. I mean, I see a bar.

*Pause.*

So, would you say you take care of people for a night or two? Do you feed them, ever?

MANAN: What do you want?

MESSENGER: To eat? That's kind of you. Do you have meat?

MANAN: You can have some of what we're having. Is that all right?

*The messenger takes off his boots.*

MESSENGER: What do you have for aching feet! I could use a bath.

*Pause.*

MANAN: I would like you to take a bath.

*The messenger rises, smiling.*

MESSENGER: What, you don't like my scent?

MANAN:

MESSENGER *(to the drunk)*: Doesn't like my scent. My kind isn't appealing. *(to the manan)* That's adrenaline you smell. What's a matter, you don't like adrenaline?

MANAN:

MESSENGER: Are we monkeying around?

DRUNK:

MANAN: Remain kind, please.

*Pause.*

MESSENGER: Yes, well, just what are the rules here?

MANAN: The rules?

MESSENGER: Yes...Back home, we knew what the rules were. Right? It was clear. Oh, those were some times, weren't they! Do you even remember? I would say those were some times, and Samara was a *good place*. And, who knows, maybe it will be good again...

MANAN:

MESSENGER: But here. It's less clear. To me. So yes. What are the rules, here?

*Pause.*

Are they the same, sirrah?

MANAN: Yes.

MESSENGER: I have no idea what got you into this debt. But it's a problem. It's nagging. I know. Because it's just something that will not go away.

MANAN:

MESSENGER: Do you want to tell me?

MANAN:

MESSENGER *(to the drunk)*: Do you want to tell me, sirrah?

DRUNK: No.

*Pause.*

The rains will come soon. The roads will wash out and the river will grow.

MESSENGER: I know.

DRUNK: I thought maybe not being from around here, you didn't know.

*Pause.*

MESSENGER: I know about that.

*Pause.*

I'm not that green.

*The messenger gives the manan a list of his charges in addition to the IOU.*

MANAN: What is this?

MESSENGER: Read it. You'll know what it is if you just read it.

MANAN: Where'd you get this?

MESSENGER: Where'd I get it?

MANAN: "Prices"? What is this?

MESSENGER: I didn't have any idea it was to be this hard, coming all this way. I was told six days. And that was wrong. And you don't know what I've been through. That's why I made it.

MANAN: That's why you made it up.

*Pause.*

"Travel, per mile: Five cents. Salary: One dollar per day. Food: Twenty-five cents per day. Wear and Tear." What's that?

MESSENGER: It means damage, sirrah.

MANAN: "...Depreciation: One dead horse. Pain and suffering:"—

DRUNK: —What's the sum?

MANAN: Seven hundred dollars.

DRUNK: Seven hundred dollars!

MESSENGER: I brought this paper to you. Eleven days!

MANAN: Well, these are your prices.

MESSENGER: *I* decide what it costs.

MANAN: Well, I don't agree.

MESSENGER: That's what it costs.

MANAN: Well, I don't recognize these prices.

*Pause.*

*(to the drunk)* What do you think?

DRUNK: Way too—

MESSENGER: —I decide the cost!

MANAN: I don't recognize these prices.

MESSENGER: I brought this to you! I had success in bringing it to you! That's a cost by itself!! I AM THE MESSENGER FROM SAMARA.

# Scene 6

*The following day. The drunk and the messenger are alone. The drunk has been drinking. The messenger is clipping his toenails.*

DRUNK: You're kind of a bully...You know that?

MESSENGER:

DRUNK: I don't mind really, I deal with bullies. I dealt with them. My father always told me how to deal with them. He said, when you look at them. He said, when you—if they bother you, you just...aw, you're not really listening to me.

MESSENGER: You say there were people in the past who wanted to beat your ass?

DRUNK:

MESSENGER: You stood up to bullies, sirrah?

DRUNK:

MESSENGER: I think it's more interesting you get beyond thinking about how you seem to others. You want to seem like the kind that doesn't like to get pushed around, BUT. You get pushed around, still.

*Pause.*

It's more interesting to be honest with what you are.

DRUNK: And what is that?

MESSENGER: You get pushed around. If it wasn't me pushing, it would be someone else.

DRUNK:

MESSENGER: It might as well be me, sirrah.

DRUNK: I don't think so. I don't need to push people around. I just live my life.

*Pause.*

When you feel power...

MESSENGER: Hey?

DRUNK: When you feel power, what is it that you're tapping into?

MESSENGER:

*Pause.*

DRUNK: I don't need power.

*Pause.*

I don't need your power, anyways.

*Pause.*

MESSENGER: True power? Is that what you're asking? True power, is in the mind.

DRUNK: Really? That's what you think?

MESSENGER: Yes.

DRUNK: It's not a feeling?!

MESSENGER: I can feel it when I want to.

*Pause.*

DRUNK: You think it's—the mind?

*Pause.*

But, you're not really getting down there! You think you are?!...But you're resting at a level above it, hovering above it. Where you are? You're not even close. You need to descend, dude— Find a way! To get down deeper, open up the body to more circuits, more avenues, capillaries. Open, breathe, open. You'll open and descend...

*Pause.*

MESSENGER: You're going the wrong way, sirrah.

DRUNK: Nah!

MESSENGER: You're supposed to *a*-scend. Not *de*-scend.

DRUNK: No!

MESSENGER: The heavens, get it? Up?

DRUNK: Not the heavens. Down. The earth and below. You know all these things of like. You should take all of the here and now, this world. Right. That's what I meant...You know, the fear of death is *(belching) verrry* powerful...

MESSENGER: You sirrah, are grotesque.

DRUNK:

*Pause.*

MESSENGER: Tell me what your father said, if you don't mind.

DRUNK: Said what? Oh, you don't care. He said, confront them. Avoid the fight by all means, and then...if still they persist...

MESSENGER: Yes?

DRUNK: You know...

MESSENGER: No. Tell me.

*The drunk regards the messenger and turns his palms face up.*

# Scene 7

*Several nights later. The drunk and the manan meet.*

MANAN: What are we gonna do?

DRUNK: I don't know.

MANAN: Every day, it gets closer to the season, he's really not leaving! The rains come and he's stuck here with us for months. He can eat, too...

DRUNK:

MANAN: Come on, help. What can we do?

DRUNK: I don't know.

MANAN:

DRUNK: He is a jerk.

*Pause.*

MANAN: You know, you're bigger than him.

DRUNK: And you're bigger than me!

MANAN:

DRUNK: You do owe the money.

MANAN: I know that! Why don't you say something that hasn't been said!

DRUNK: Well...

MANAN: It's all been said?

*Pause.*

I can make a bill, too.

*The drunk looks on while the manan completes the total.*

"Time: Hours at inn...Room: Seventeen days...Meals: Fifty-one... Whiskey. Taxes: Land, property. Water."...What else?

DRUNK: How much is that?

MANAN: Two hundred thousand.

DRUNK: I like the sound of that!

*The messenger enters.*

MANAN: You're up awful late.

MESSENGER: Just wanted to check and see how things are coming along with your payment.

MANAN: I'm just working on your bill so far...Have a seat.

MESSENGER: Thank you.

*The manan brings the bill to the messenger. The messenger reads the bill in silence. He puts it on the bar.*

FORGET that!

MANAN: I'll be mercenary just like you.

MESSENGER: Evidently! When you pay mine, I'll pay yours! Meanwhile...

*The messenger puts his hat over his eyes and puts his boots up. The manan and the drunk speak out of earshot of the messenger.*

DRUNK: Oh!

MANAN: You know. Forget this guy!

DRUNK: I wish your father was here.

MANAN:

DRUNK: Yep, he should be here. Someone should. I wish—I wish we had the money. I just wish we had it, that's all.

MANAN: When is he gonna leave?

DRUNK: I wish Hill would come and clear it all away. Clear this problem right away.

*Rain is falling.*

And here come the rains!

MANAN: Get rid of this guy.

*Pause.*

If I could just scare him. If I got Dad's gun?

*The drunk goes to get the gun.*

DRUNK: With Hilton's gun?

MANAN: Yeah, I could do that.

DRUNK: You want to do that?

MANAN: With that?

DRUNK: You mean with this?

*The drunk pulls a shining rifle out from its velvet purse. The metal gleams.*

MANAN: That's something right there.

DRUNK: Does he have a gun?

MANAN: Nah!

DRUNK: You better be sure.

MANAN: You see how every day he goes out after supper?

DRUNK: Yeah, what's he doing?

MANAN: I'll be waiting for him in the twilight.

## Scene 8

*The next night, after supper. The manan is inspecting the rifle when the messenger comes into the room. The manan, surprised, springs up and points the gun at the messenger's face.*

MESSENGER: No!

*The manan shoots the messenger dead.*

MANAN: NO! Ah! Oh my God! No! NO!!...I hope you know, this was not my intention.

# Scene 9

*The drunk is digging a hole while the manan looks on. The body of the messenger is lying behind them under a blood-soaked sheet.*

MANAN: What now?

DRUNK: Bury the body.

*Day becomes night. In darkness, the manan places a hand on the messenger's heart. The drunk finishes digging and grabs ahold of the messenger's feet. The manan stops him.*

MANAN: I can't leave him here! Will you help me?

DRUNK: Help you what?

MANAN: Take him back.

DRUNK: Back. What is back?

MANAN: Take him home.

DRUNK: NO!

MANAN: We have to. It's the only way.

DRUNK: Where??

MANAN: You know the path.

DRUNK: I came all this way, I don't want to go back.

MANAN: So we stay stuck out here?

DRUNK:

MANAN: Look. I'm stuck, too! I'm sorry. I can't leave him. Help me take him back!

*The manan holds the cold body of the messenger. The drunk goes and picks up the manan. After a moment*:

Please! It's a trip a person hopes to make only once but I'm asking you to take it with me.

# Scene 10

*Later that night. The drunk talks to himself in the dark, with the torn-up map.*

DRUNK: Go through this..."New-found-land." Can you do it? It's longer. Is it possible?...Home. Psh. That's just the name of a place you leave and don't ever go back to. Go as far as you can...Take a look at the fucken map here, genius. Look...you see that this is land right? That's you right there. Now. See this? That's water. Show me how to get to home without crossing this fucking body of water, asshole.

*Pause. The drunk gets up and walks to the messenger's body.*

Damn! After fifty years, a man has got to realize that he is living on top of a fence. He begins by thinking he knows what it all means, and what he should do. Then, he becomes sure what it all means and what he should do, and apologizes for what he thought it meant and all the things that he did do. Later on, he puts what he *should* do against the things he really *wants* to do. And now. Why can't he complete a sentence without stuttering, or flubbing a word, not able to say anything without running through it in his mind. To see how it will sound. It is pure fear. Fear and sound, can't bring them together. What's going to happen to him? What is the fence dividing? Old and new? Pleasure and duty? Life, death? Good bad? Known unknown?...COME DOWN OFF THE FENCE!!... Oh, I'm comin down off the fence...Thank God.

*The drunk wakes the manan.*

MANAN: What?

DRUNK: Ok.

# Scene 11

*The drunk and the manan depart. Following old codes, they carry the messenger over the pass, through the river and its difficult current. When they dry off, they go on, finding higher land and beyond that, more hills. They traverse. They descend, they ascend. The manan and the drunk travel back whence the messenger came. They are propelled forward to a place of rest, and, at the top of one of these hills, the drunk's knees give out.*

DRUNK: Ahhh!

*The manan crouches over, attempts to rise the drunk. The drunk doesn't respond. The manan stands, then fruitlessly tries to lift the body of the messenger.*

MANAN: I'll keep you close to my heart. In my fantasy, I broke it all off and kept my allegiance to only myself. And in this new fantasy, it begins. When you keep allegiance to yourself and only yourself, you never lie, you never let people down.

*The manan leaves the drunk and the body of the messenger behind.*

# Scene 12

*The Outskirts. Sounds of trucks roaring in the distance. The radio-relay towers join phone-relay towers, red joined by white light.*

*The manan traverses an old golf course at dusk, and, at dawn finds a rest stop bathroom. Fluorescent light. Dripping sounds. The feeling of the vastness just outside and the highway extending. The manan continues along the perimeter where the sounds are the echoes of the night and the manan experiences exterior and interior overlapping.*

*Far off and traveling in the opposite direction, two men approach with their mother, Agnes. Agnes is small and seemingly from another time, the men are shirtless and sweaty. One of the men is a beast of a man. They carry a bag of tools, including a machete, knife, rope, bat, a gun, and a hammer.*

AGNES *(as she approaches)*: You don't want to talk to me, but I'm making you talk to me...And I can feel it even if you don't say it! You don't want me to tell you— (I can't tell you anything.) I'm not attacking you, son. If I was attacking you I would say you're a fuck-up. Am I saying you're a fuck-up? I'm saying that I don't like where this is going and I want to know what's going on with you. You need to tell me how you feel! That's all I'm asking.

COWBOY: Two sides to every story, Ma.

*Agnes spots the manan.*

AGNES: Hello, stranger.

*The beast runs ahead, the cowboy right behind him.*

COWBOY: Shit...

AGNES: Get him...

*The cowboy clips one beast ankle into the other. The beast falls on the ground. The cowboy holds the beast down with his chest.*

Come, sit down, don't pay any attention to them. Come on, come on.

MANAN:

AGNES: Tell us who you are. Come on.

MANAN: Ah.

AGNES: What gives here. Where do you come from. What's your name.

*The beast proceeds to inspect the stranger. The cowboy looks on. Silence.*

MANAN: Uh, got lost...trying to find the highway.

AGNES: Where you goin?

MANAN: Um, to see a vendor.

COWBOY: What's that?

MANAN: A "vendor"?

COWBOY: Yeah.

AGNES: Vendor is someone that sells things.

COWBOY: What did they sell you? Why not just say seller, Ma?

MANAN: Uh...

AGNES: Look at the man's eyes. There is great pain there, do you see it? The way he's breathin, see?! Look at his chest. You see it moving? Look how he doesn't check his breath? Hello there old soul. You see, this is a deep man.

BEAST: You're deep too, Ma.

COWBOY *(to the manan)*: This Ms. Agnes.

AGNES: Well sit, there, sit! And we'll call it a day. Boys, set up.

*The boys gather kindling wood and set up a little camp and prepare food over a fire.*

Sometimes I lose my temper with them and I always regret that. They're not in the same frame of mind as I. I have to remember that. And I'm not always right. That's something, to always recognize that. But I feel like I have to say what I have to say, and let them work it out if I go too far. You forgive me for that, right?

MANAN: Sure.

AGNES: Like ciphers. Love them. The ground beneath me shifts and hardens, concrete below. It also loosens and gives way. That old man said he loves her when he's with her, and loves me when he's with me. That ain't gonna work. An ever-changing foundation, beneath the feet. And now there's only two. My youngest is missing. They said he went this route to deliver a message. He been gone too long, it's time to bring him home.

*Agnes pulls out a photo.*

On your path from wherever you came from, did you see this boy?

MANAN: Your son was a messenger...

AGNES: My son *is* a messenger.

MANAN:

AGNES: Well. You tell me what you're doing out here.

MANAN: Oh, I wish I knew...I owe something, and I have to pay it back.

AGNES: So what's the plan? You gonna pay it? Can you pay it?

MANAN: I want to, yes. I'm on my way to pay it back.

AGNES: Where?

MANAN: I don't know. I'll start in Samara.

AGNES: Who do you owe it to.

MANAN: Huh. I'm not sure.

AGNES: Ha! Well you're headed toward Samara anyways.

MANAN: That was my intention. I'll start with my father. I guess that's where it started.

AGNES: You owe your father?

MANAN: Well...

AGNES: Why don't you talk? You have a cagey method of conversing. It's irritating. Sit down.

*The manan sits.*

MANAN: I had a partner. We traveled far together. But I had to let that go...I slipped and I slided...this was not my intention...My father. He wanted to be all things to all people. I was awed by him. I couldn't live up to what he created. And neither could he. But I imagine the smallest thing...Like, he never said he loved me but I didn't care. Because he knew that to say it meant something else.

*Day becomes night.*

You called me a man.

AGNES: Well, so? That's what you are, aren't you?

MANAN: I could very well be.

AGNES: That's what you seem to me.

MANAN: Well. If I'm a man, I'm a bad one.

AGNES: I haven't met any good ones...

*The boys clean up. The cowboy unpacks the bed stuffs, circles the fire.*

MANAN: I should write all this down, this trip. The things I've seen!

AGNES: Like what? Tell me!

COWBOY: What have you seen? Nice things?

MANAN: No! But I like to look back at what I've seen all the same. Visit it again.

BEAST: Tell it.

MANAN: What can I say...I've seen old land, wild land. I can still see pagan and enchanted time, back to Arab time. Uncontrollable desires, relieved and saved, held by, barely contained by God, and magic never quite quelled. Pulled by the ecstasies of the body and physical world. How could I want so much, demand so much and expect so much for so little. There is incredible pleasure out there. It exists. I've seen it. But you cannot live there. Life is not pleasure. You cannot stay. It's a world for the unenlightened.

AGNES: You can't take energy away. It takes a lot to get something to change direction. But it's been my experience that if you can find that place, stay there. I like things up in the air like that.

*The boys are asleep.*

MANAN: Thank you, ma'am, for your kindness. I'll be on my way.

AGNES: Stay.

*The manan approaches and beds down next to Agnes.*

I raised them in concrete. Gave that old man the slip. We don't blame anybody. Because both knew staying there would be suicide. Your foundation is under your feet. Always. Meanwhile, wild desire exists above, from above, some will argue, somewhere in the sky. A pursuit begins because of the interior lack. The boys are good company. Look at that beast. He grew big too fast. All this has worn me out. I gotta get a new hip. Gotta get a new back. Everything. Ohhh. It doesn't stop. This kind of health—it's in the family.

*The rain has stopped. There isn't much left in words around this fire. Later, after the boys are asleep, Agnes reaches over to the manan and whispers:*

What about you? Could you change direction?

*The manan rolls on top of her. They make love in the night.*

*While they are sleeping around the fire, the manan sits unmoved, wide awake.*

*There is a dull breaking up of the night.*

*The drunk appears, carrying the body of the messenger.*

*The drunk places the body on the ground.*

*The manan rises when he sees the drunk. The manan and the drunk look at each other and the drunk falls next to the manan.*

*Dawn arrives. The family wakes up and the beast first goes to the body. The manan has not moved. The beast is cautious in the gloom, circling the sleeping drunk.*

COWBOY *(to the manan)*: Who are you?

*The drunk is awake but frozen with fear, eyes closed.*

AGNES: WHAT IS THIS?

DRUNK: I'm scared, G...

MANAN: I'm scared, too!

*The drunk stands. The family watches as the beast lifts the shroud covering his dead brother. The beast, afraid, not knowing who to turn to, looks up with pleading eyes. The beast tries to shake the messenger awake. The cowboy is stuck in place.*

It was me...IT WAS FUCKEN ME!

*Pause.*

BEAST: "Me"...What does that mean, "me"?...

COWBOY:

BEAST: What does that mean, "me"?

COWBOY:

BEAST: WHAT DOES THAT MEAN, "ME"!!!

*The manan turns to the beast.*

MANAN: I'm exactly where I'm supposed to be.

*The beast rushes the manan. The cowboy ropes the foot of the beast, then grabs the hammer, hitting him. The cowboy exhibits brave strength in subduing the beast, but the beast pulls loose, raving. The mother grabs the bat and joins in. The drunk steps in and has the beast in a chokehold from behind. The beast is sobbing. The mother walks over to her dead son and pets his head.*

*There they lie, holding each other, and let it be plain: this will be known as pure love. Nothing less, and absolute.*

AGNES *(sings)*:

Sleep in peace my precious one
In between the moon and sun
Roof of velvet bed of stone
Wood and river blood and bone
Lay you down in sweet repose
Heath and heather for your clothes

Aster, bluebell, bramble rose
Asphodel and clover

Hush a bye my darlin son
Mama's here the monsters gone
All your wanderin is done
Respite only just begun
There's no need for you to rise
Rest you easy close your eyes
Dream a dream of paradise
Seraphs sailing over

Elysium, Elysium
Over in Elysium
Toil and trouble never come
Over in Elysium

Sleep in peace my precious one
In between the moon and sun
Roof of velvet bed of stone
Wood and river blood and bone

*Agnes turns to the group:*

Back to the old country...Shot through memory holes...Yeah. He
owes them a culture. He stole it. They want their culture back.
He contained it in his core. He brought it away from its source.
He failed to bring it out in the new environment and his thicken-
ing flesh prevented breath and it sat inside him to fester. Now he
owes. A whole culture.

*(to the manan)* You. You owe.

*Agnes exits.*

*I really want to tell you it was a beautiful ceremony. If reeds could be extrapolated out from the chanter and into the wilderness, and true power was rooted in the drone; this made for a most moving ceremony for a burying. The bodies without words are left to do the explaining, for a situation that doesn't require explanation. Even light, spread with a warm glow but with unusual clarity. Dusk again touching into that place where all memory waits to be recognized. You could return.*

# Scene 13

*Looking over the green trees from the air, a bird flew southerly and yet the swath of growth had latitude too, so much that it dizzied any head but hers. She flew and flew.*

*The brain of the bird was of course not aware of any of this, it was operating on directives, inside, without any awareness of any operation, listening in. The trees disappeared as night fell and the bird flew on in darkness still, until allowing herself to be pulled down by wind, and found the right branch at the top of a white tree.*

*There, she made adjustments, and finding adequate darkness on a branch under the top, she fell quickly asleep, comfortable because of thoughts of other birds that were her friends. Now, look at her. Her dark eyes; the lip came down and up leaving a little tiny beak of a smile, a dull and thorough end to the day.*

*This bird, like the rest, woke up with the first sign of darkness giving way.*

*And you. The bird sees you, and continues on her way. So you are left on the edge of a forest hunting in the morning. You have foregone so much to be here in this forest today. You survive living without a tribe, a family, or companion. Of course, your days are numbered.*

*Your general understanding of forest guides you through unfamiliar terrain. You know where berries will grow, which bark to eat, and where game will be; your body is your keel, carrying you and your second nature, undaunted and unceremonious.*

*Look, you've caught a hare. Look, you speared a fish. Look there, you're wading in cold water. You see, your days are filled up, no problem... You tug on a filament, tomorrow you will chip out an arrowhead. In* the fastnesses, you wake with the sun and do not stop moving until darkness comes in again.

Take a look at your face. Your features are not anomalous anywhere in the continent of upper Asia, or Northern America. You are ancient man. Back to frozen continents and deep caverns of ice with endless mass, height: frightening. You are a special warrior, a warrior without ego. You wander the continent, not sad, but walking in the absence of joy. You have burned off all your hair in mourning for your family. You haven't been able to use any dying words out loud. But the bird knows you whisper them in the nighttime.

You know that by stopping being busy you will cease to exist. Sadness chases you, nips at your heels, ever-present, but ever-managed.

Do you see the three ages of man repeat?

I see how candied builders and pillars lapse into complacent control, invariably: comfort, status and respect, proceeding regardless. In the face of so much violence and time, here's children asking questions. Here's a meeting of young women—their thirsty hands of hope and possibility and purpose filling them up to the eyes. Here's an old man teaching songs to be remembered. Why worry when this is possible. And, how is this possible?

The forest is what is under foot and supports you. The landscape is impossibly green and expands forever in every direction. You walk for weeks, and months, not seeing a soul. How did you survive for so long?

Meanwhile, the bird she climbs and she finds. She also finds the violence and time, and for her it's just something to get by. The charm of this bird, indifferent to all our concerns. She flies, and finds how two halves collide. The lies from two sides and she traces a line from high country to the divide and the bird climbs.

# Scene 14

*Wake up, baby.*

*Taking the gravel driveway back here in the dark, rolling over it with headlights, jerking the black like entering the mouth of a great beast.*

*Push the car door open past the door check. The buzz comes on until you take out the keys and drop them in the plastic dash.*

*Come on, let's go.*

*Our eyes adjust. The moon is up. The meadow is on the right. It's bright enough that you can make out a color or two. We rent it out so it's always just something pretty to look at. There is a satisfying scale to it from where we stand on the raised road; the waves of it, the lazy bends in it, and the shadow-marked bails of rolled-up grass.*

*The stars see us.*

*Look up, sweetheart. A shooting star, whoa. Too late.*

"Wow. That was fast!"

*She stares up at the sky, waiting. With just her presence she seems to say, "Sure, any place you like," and, "It's great." She comes to a spot, a place, and it's like she's planted in the ground. This girl, who can see the insides of things.*

*A sound sputters in the gully. Then the shape of something big moves on the left side of the road.*

"What is it?"

*I don't know.*

*"I'm scared," she says and takes my hand.*

*What you see may not be there, it's just the dark playing tricks, sweetheart. It's probably just a deer.*

*"Are you scared?" she asks.*

*Oh yeah.*

*(Actually, I can't remember the last time I was scared of the dark. I miss it.)*

*"I'm scared."*

*Don't worry. Maybe it's a lost cow. Whatever it is…he'll work his side of the street and we'll work ours.*

*She looks out with genuine wonder.*

*A horse clambers up onto the road, wild and injured. He clumsily tries to gallop ahead of us and then labors out of sight.*

*"Is that a horse?" she asks.*

*It sure is.*

*"Whose is it?"*

*Don't know. Never seen it before.*

*We come around a bend and see the horse try to come out of itself—the weight of it toppling as it goes. I'm thinking, Who will I call about this?*

*"What's wrong with him?"*

I don't know, sweetheart.

*"Will he die?" she asks.*

Not sure.

*"What if he dies?"*

He may.

*"What does it mean?"*

If he dies? That will mean his body has stopped working.

*"Like when your phone dies?"*

No. Not like that.

*"Why?"*

Because you can't recharge it.

She thinks for a moment as I look down at her and then back at the purposeless horse getting away from us down the road.

*"You can't get it back?"*

No, you can't.

*"Why?" And she starts to cry.*

Nobody knows.

*"You don't come back??"*

*Come on now. Let's keep going. All you can do is believe what will happen.*

*We walk down the face of the bluff. Come out from under tree cover and feel black water cooling the air around the lake. The moon lights up the surface. A breeze blows the leaves in some parts. Silence is all around us.*

*She wants me to pick her up.*

*Nah, you can walk.*

*"I'm cold!"*

*All right! For old times' sake.*

*She clutches my back.*

*We continue along in light that makes everything seem like a negative of what it is.*

*With her in my arms I climb back up onto that stretch, that over-arching pass.*

*From here, you start to see how interstate turned to state, state turned to county, county turned to gravel and now gravel is just a path, just two tracks of mud with a strip of grass in between. Finds us miles from where we began. The old road. They say these old tracks used to join two bona fide towns.*

*Up on the rise we turn.*

*That's back where we came from. See?*

*She looks, then lays her head flat on my shoulder.*

*This road and this tree, leaves shimmy in the breeze. Its cutout shape is defined by the sky behind. This whole piece of land is known, its impression is fossilized on the backside of the brain because it's been the most constant thing in my life. And its innocent presence has seeped into the subconscious, and it says "Home." The road, the garage, the barn, the house. The neighbors along that stretch of road.*

*But take that slice out of the earth and examine it completely. Look at the whole thing. It's earth that changes hands. It has not an ounce of inherent dignity. There is no home here anymore.*

*No more shrines, no more memorials. Let the past recede. Be like water flow and no identity now and further on and history gone. And turn the page.*

*And your water joins the music out there and becomes the eternal everlasting hereafter streams of no time, and melt all elements and then everything is possible and where to go, forever on the edge of becoming, without power.*

*You can knock me down...*

*If you want...I have no power.*

*It's this point of departure now. Like a hole in your pocket where a token might drop, or half a crown.*

*I like to run over in my mind, that time and the lines leading up to a face, and dulcet singing.*

*And wake up with the bright sun opening up on that same piece and it doesn't seem possible that these two pieces are in fact the same.*

# Scene 15

*The set takes over in the silence. It changes its shape. Eventually, the lights are slowly taken out, as the set begins to move and maneuver. Platforms rise up and breathe. In the dark, there is only the sound of moving parts.*

Paradiso

*A white pickup truck comes out of the night and into the room, muffled music blasting from its sound system. Passengers can be made out through the tinted glass. The engine is cut, the music goes out, and a robot exits the truck, processing his surroundings. The robot arrives at a spot in front of the audience.*

ROBOT: Air quiet all around us. The tilt of the zodiac and four bright stars have emerged. Same coordinates, different map. Stand on the earth, here, on this spot at night and look up at the sky. The stars so thick, brings to mind Shelley's *Hymn to Apollo*: "Curtained with star-inwoven tapestries." And these vestiges from old thoughts waft up, shoulda-woulda thoughts, like: What if we knew about the natural gas reserves hidden in buried tanks for just such a situation. What if we knew the portals were real, where they held huge caches of life-giving auras and fresh water. Would that have saved us? Man, let that go, too haphazard to maintain any equilibrium anyway.

Look up now: a black so clean it has no surface or depth. It's just plain absence...Let's watch the movement of lightness into dark and back to light...There is still this "present moment," you feel it, right? And there is still this place, this ground still underfoot. Even from the point of view of the now-defunct supernatural, the thinly veiled spirit world that once was, where shades once repped the people who once were, there is still this ground beneath us. And what was the word for waves in the sea, and clouds in the sky?

In a minute, we're gonna talk about love, but isn't this just too incredible right now? C'mon. Let's take this in...Walk the world alone with us...

Welcome to the play, by the way. The nice thing about the play is it makes a place wherever we gather: make a semi-circle on the floor, make some rows, whatever; wherever we can see each other. This is where you go when there's no place to go, or place to put ideas that otherwise would just float in space.

...We were at war. A twenty-year-plus war with no end in sight. What did that feel like? Well, don't ask the universe. Like a human's eye view of the frantic ant colony, such was the cosmic view of human warfare; the utterly neutral cosmos (which is not the same as God) said, "Man either will or won't carry on in some fashion—what do we care if it's Muslim, Christo-Judeo, or Zoro-astrianism??"

For old times' sake, let's briefly draw out some elements of Earth. I have three or four remarkable locales in mind...

One is palagonite mountains and basalt, and after the reptilian ridges, and depth of field, the green lacing, fading lines of the hills into silhouette, and blending or taking on the sky, yet still with shape; lazy slopes, scooped piles dumped, and settled into what we called beauty, perfection, personal freedom: everything with a natural explanation. Let's take this gradual, easy decline...The reason the rocks are different kinds is they got made at different temperatures.

And now look, this water, isn't this interesting: the water has an uncut, glassy look that should only signify cleanliness, healthfulness, a geometry that comes from geology, harkening the affair between Gaea and Pontus. This water is a river wanting to be an ocean. It still has that playful bounce of a kid wanting to be a man and just as poignant, because while you root for it, you can't help thinking: you're a dirty river, you'll never amount to anything. The Indians had a name for you that means something like "travels in both directions."

...And over here, this place here: sun sun and sun, blue blue and blue, desperate blue. Sand, flats of sand, more sand, now, flats of sand. And the sun dries anything it can find, including the fluid in your eyeballs. Including you. Dry sand and sand and sand. If you ever wanted exile, this was the place.

Long term we were never gonna make it out here. We needed each other, and yet we were often alone and wouldn't see each other again...Thinking about the past and I wonder if you would just imagine, or remember: Love has no merit nor no blame, love is love...

It's behind us...we turn away.

*Paradiso*, by R. M.

**1**

*Elaine exits the truck.*

ELAINE: Lest you think this be some morbid jag, I want to tell you right up top that it can't. "Morbid" is a living person's idea; it's not morbid to the dead. After all, what is our death compared to light that took twenty-four thousand years to get here? Or these rocks, for example. So already let go of any idea that we can survive because we can't. We have run forward, eliminating the line marking death, and love is all that remains.

Absorbed into it, we make up the darkness, or cause it, from this hulking mass we create, throwing long shadows...I enjoy the cover. When we were alive, I enjoyed the cover of nature: say fog, or dim light and perhaps a slope made of eroded earth with purplish, dusky hues. Now I enjoy this other cover. And now reflect on what love is, or was, but I think *is*, because love never needed us, and knows no rules. Were you surprised by your love of "the other"? Now that you can see it from the outside. (Love is not beauty after all.)

It was said seismic events always happen in threes. But then found they also happened in fours, fives and sixes, if you were willing to wait for it.

Was death any solace? Survival did make me uncomfortable: all the conflicted feelings, mixed emotions, and morality. As I look around at the countryside with no one in it, from all these angles and positions, I see the traces of people motoring themselves around, and the immediate gratification, and or the glorification that soaked us all in; I end up with a vision of the multitudes who knew how to do only this one thing.

Among all the justifiable feelings, I felt relief when a loved one died, as the death allows the suspension to end. Balanced out by, and hopefully overcome by, feeling of faith and active prayer that they will live.

But hey, I can talk about survival. Because despite the odds, we did find love in the family, and it was a real thing, that wasn't just base, selfish needs. And it kept us going, no denying it...

Family. I adored them, but turns out that was only partly the point. Push-pull for much of our lives: until I said I felt like she didn't like me, she hadn't said she adored me. This kind of personal stuff was not trivial in our family. This feeling that could exist between people was ordinary, fraught, combustible. You couldn't see it except from the inside, all mauled by an eviscerating beast that didn't know itself. Felt responsible, no matter what I did. The people you cared about also wanted you to be real with them, but then you realized they just meant be self-effacing. And, the threat of unforgiveness was the nuclear option you always assumed on the table. An incalculable flinging of emotional stars; it was less hazardous to stay away.

But, see, we didn't have to be the same way on things. Once I accepted that, and let go of any guilt from years of giving the, not really the cold shoulder, but more becoming absorbed in myself, I tried to be in touch. To be around. Which was tricky, because you had to know when you were welcome or not, because they wouldn't tell you. But I was surprised, as I drove away from her house with her in it, I thought to myself: this is what love looks like. Just try to be there more. And fail. And hurtle through unoccupied zones. And wait, and hope and pray for that turnaround: when it will be all right??

I could only hope to come to understand her, not from my perspective, not from anyone else's, but from her eyes.

*"Rich, I wanna go."*

I went over to her bedside. You want to go to the toilet?

*"I want you to call Nurse Betty, tell her. I want her to knock me out."*

She was always very good at resisting anything mythic about being a mother: For swimmer's itch, *"Use bicarbonate of soda and a wet washcloth."*

Now we're alone, and I see her true character is unbreakable till the end. On the night she died, she says, *"Cancel Sharon. She's supposed to clean tomorrow."*

She tells me, *"That anger is going to kill you. It also hurts you creatively."*

That stays, somehow. What fades or what needs support are the things that are taken for granted: open those blinds and you see cropped, balding grass, browning, shedding hydrangea bushes, a paved driveway, walkways, the clothesline, the flagpole, the leaning vacant birdhouse, the broken birdbath, the bird feeders, the marigolds, the wooden planters...The sky isn't blue. It's neither overcast nor sunny—it's a white slate that blanks your eyes across the day and it daily worsens. Visibility drops and the smoke can be seen hanging lower and you think, Maybe we're on fire. The sky turns green. The distant roar of the wall cloud, turning vertical, comes close. She has a tablet in her lap and follows the radar. We have bumped her down the stairs in the wheelchair and now hole up in the back bedroom. The kids are excited, jumping on the bed. My brother and I, with Dolores in tow, steal looks upstairs at the churning sky and the rain starts, and the trees are dancing. The storm passes. I have to wheel her outside to get back upstairs. Up the hillside, she gets an unexpected tour of the yard and surrounding woods. In a half voice: *"Mmm...it's beautiful."* This is her domain, which hasn't been available to her for months, and I recall her only one year earlier, touring her garden patches on foot, sidling up and down the hillside pondering, studying, righting herself and picking at weeds. I push her up the hill, which brings me closer to her white hair: I don't want to miss a word. We reach the front of the house, the best side, with the tall windows of different four-sided shapes. The sky is breaking up, showing cracks of blue: "*Oh...we were spared. Praise the Lord.*" And among broken branches and flower stems on the ground: "*So pretty.*"

She knew we were coming to say goodbye. And she would never stand in the way of anyone's good time. Did I get to turn over all the stones I wanted?

After a certain number of hours together, past the point where you feel the other judging you; and past the point of counting time altogether, you find all that matters is you need them and don't know what you would do without them and yet, when they go, you manage, because that feeling continues.

And maybe you got to the bottom of an inflection, to that place you always assumed other families got to, in their own.

. . . . . .

Brittle woods

Loons wail

3:30 a.m.

. . . . . .

*Carina, Charlie and Jessica fall out of the truck.*

# Scene

*Time: The moment of mammal gaining legs and touching shore, to leave the sea behind.*

*Place: Shoreline.*

*The animals in pristine nature.*

*An epic deer tale in the woods, with orchestral excitement.*

*Lines coming back swinging out and back on six points: a way of answering.*

*Looking for free space.*

*Use desert and night to get there.*

# Scene

*Time: 2015.*

*Place: Limbus Farm.*

*Happy refuge. Forty years of labor, daily chores, getting the kids to the bus, weathering winters. We are often depressed, looking for distinction within and without our lives.*

*There are two, two-car garages. One dates to 1989. The other, 1996.*

*In sister Peggy's garage there are Larry's tools and machinery, bicycles, and Simpsons character pinups, printouts on dot-matrix paper. Neil Young/Beck tickets nailed to a stud. There is a stereo with a tape deck,* stopped in the middle of the last tape Larry played before he died. R.E.M.'s _____ .

It is exactly as it was in 1998.

In the other garage are Pa's tools, and lawn/gardening equipment, his riding mower, some high-jump equipment including a crash pad and bar. File cabinet full of manila folders of news clippings and memorabilia, carvings he made, lawn chairs Mom found on the cheap. A croquet set. A few water toys and life jackets and paddles. A bookcase full of dusty books.

Peggy is the de facto guardian of this place. This is Limbus Farm. Both garages, both houses. The land. A memento.

Mom, last breaths on her bed.

The adrenaline rush of, don't lie, relief. Of peace, in general. Grief comes later.

## Scene

Time:

Place: Desert.

Picture a desert, and we're in the middle of it. It's day. The sky is searing blue. We may travel along the horizon. We may travel by way of winding up, to these gaps. The sun plus desert is an absence and is all. The destroyed temples. A civil war where everybody died.

Lightning separated out from thunder and sky, cracks right overhead. Electricity tosses bodies to the earth.

# Scene

*Time: 2014.*

*Place:*

*Forces push the wind out and clip the feet. An enemy is sicked and cannot be beaten. Cruel inequity reigns, but all dreams are kept equal and share legitimacy. All this shit from the world: people's heads get cut off and we drown and starve, and get beaten down, and we will never not be at war. What choice is there? What kind of religion? Fuck it, I can't dwell on it, I have to move on...*

*We are special people caring for children since the time of stone smashing the chaff from the wheat. In the most impoverished and naked suffering, you still find people caring for kids and carrying on. We are loving.*

# Scene

*Time: Near the end of rational thought. A mother's death, against a landscape of war.*

*Place: A kind of proving ground, with the mother exalted, having achieved great status as a warrior.*

*"Green wings cleave the air."...The garden...rivulet, bending grass...A pleasant breeze.*

*Paradise means to be with the people you love who you lost, to reside in all the energy and vitality of hope. To go where time is an endless summer. The lives and the circling needs, as they stand now, the shape of lakes and swells and smoothed land reconstituted for us as we depart.*

*"Here root of mankind was innocent, here is always spring, and every fruit."*

# Allies

*Two travelers make camp.*

CHARLIE: You want some tea?

CARINA: Yes, please.

*Charlie puts a kettle on.*

*Pause.*

*Water boils. He pours.*

CHARLIE: Do you take milk?

CARINA: I do.

CHARLIE: Sugar?

*He adds two cubes. He stirs and hands her the cup. She sips.*

CARINA: It's good.

*They finish their tea.*

## 2

JESSICA: The train on tracks: matte sounds, syncopated. The smell of the railroad ties heating up in the sun. Early morning light rising up on grass patches and a whitetail in the yard, composed like a statue, staring and breathing, effortlessly. A cottontail loping about, while doves jockey and flutter, a redbird in the trees. The springtime warm wind gusting in, after sunshowers, passing by the ankles. The milk and honey was real. You could taste it.

Men and women crossed the ocean and braved the desert. The ocean made us seem so different. Over baked earth, what was on our backs and feet was all that we had, and without a horse we were dead for sure. Fully grown people with our whole history on them and reason for being, the sons and daughters. Lone pilgrims dying by heat, thirst, hunger, disease. They killed and cheated others to get across and make a claim. They died for what they wanted, because we wanted it too. They burned out young, but they didn't die before finding pleasure and relief after pain.

Should we have done it? What difference does it make, whatever the reasons, we beat back nature, not as heroes but as a whole: seduced, intoxicated by the wide open land with all that was inside and underneath. We wanted escape all along. And as it went, we got to see what replaced it. As it went, we saw for a fleeting moment something so vivid and full of surprise and possibility, we: handed keys to a garden we could imagine, but couldn't go back to. And each day you explored a little more, started over a little more, not sure of the rules, the rock, soil, flora, fauna, green and blue. It was love, then, to take the endless green and blue.

# Allies (continued)

CARINA: What's that smell?

CHARLIE *(smiling)*: Roasting beetroot.

CARINA: Smells good. How'd you manage that?

CHARLIE: I wrapped it in tinfoil and heated it up.

CARINA: Mmm.

CHARLIE: Also boiled some water.

*She sips.*

CARINA: It's actually not bad.

*She sips.*

Mm. A hot water party.

CHARLIE: What more do you need?

*He hands her the beet wrapped in foil.*

Yeah, careful. It's hot.

*She tastes.*

CARINA: That's really good. Thank you.

CHARLIE: Have some more. Eat.

*She eats.*

CARINA: Put your pack here when you're ready. I'll pick it up.

CHARLIE: No I got it.

CARINA: If we leave now we'll get an hour on the sun.

CHARLIE: Great.

CARINA: Weather. Not bad. Look.

*They look up.*

# 2 (continued)

JESSICA: We saw "America" and it was deemed worth dying and surviving for: made decisions to fight, knowing if taken we would be tortured or killed. We became patriots as it was deemed necessary to survive. We woke up and became engaged with our world. We tried harder, we loved better, as loving was thought something that can be taught. We returned to values of our parents, of working hard and staying true to family and community. We believed in possession, decency. We wanted people to succeed because their success helped others. Families, where the kids were protected and nurtured. We became a loving nation that recognized that not all people have the same opportunities in life and work, abundant food, security, and culture. We were tolerant so long as we felt we could do what we needed to do.

# Allies (continued)

CHARLIE: Do you want to sleep? Here.

*Charlie rolls out rug and bed.*

CARINA: Ok. Maybe so.

CHARLIE: Sure go ahead...don't mind me.

CARINA: Well...maybe. Just rest my eyes for a moment.

CHARLIE: Do you need a pillow? Let me get it. Come on lie down.

*Carina lies down.*

CARINA: Thank you.

CHARLIE: Comfortable?

CARINA: Maybe a blanket.

CHARLIE: Coming up.

*He unfurls a blanket over her.*

How about a little music? Do you like the radio? Here try this.

*He clicks on the radio.*

CARINA *(settling)*: Mmm.

CHARLIE: Relax.

CARINA: This is great, thank you.

CHARLIE: Here how about if you turn from the light because maybe it's too bright.

CARINA: No I like it.

CHARLIE: Good. Stay.

*He pats her.*

Goodnight. Have a good sleep.

CARINA: Goodnight.

# 2 (continued)

JESSICA: In time, we could define what humane meant. And once freedom had been personally defined, no one could take it away: edgy, on guard for the slightest hint of a threat. In time, we could put a stamp on notions because they didn't feel right.

People might have had conflicting feelings about their own identity but no one wanted their identity challenged because it was either what they wanted or what they were used to. The nuance of one-to-one relationships got lost and I'm guessing you didn't want to lose face either. Exasperation seeped out: as one person you shouldn't have to have a prescription for liking people. At any rate, we didn't feel fulfilled by any battle for free speech and justice; grew angry when it ate into our lives. And when we felt ourselves flit between guilt and comfort, we mostly chose the latter.

We can't fault ourselves for loving ourselves. As we jetted out toward the inside and out, saw opportunity and stepped in, defining a culture of procedure, the rules took over because no one wanted to be responsible for taking them away. Elegant and enabling platforms bought us some years of self-delusion but, in fact had an autoimmune disease from the beginning, and we realized it was better when we never had any hope of being elite.

"Oh, we were scared," you say, "we shouldn't have been scared." But you know what came after and fear can't be measured with hindsight.

Finally though, there was no accounting for desire. We ran out of havens for greed and lust and the only legitimized avenue for these uncontrollable urges, ultimately, was war.

# Allies (continued)

*Charlie wakes up.*

CARINA: What's wrong?

CHARLIE: Not sure.

CARINA: Sleep ok?

CHARLIE: Fine.

*Pause.*

I had a dream.

CARINA: Elizabeth?

CHARLIE: Yes.

CARINA: What was it?

CHARLIE: It was weird.

CARINA: Tell me.

CHARLIE: I don't know where I was. But that doesn't matter.

CARINA: Why not?

CHARLIE: Because I was listening to a phone message.

CARINA: Gotcha. What was the message?

CHARLIE: She said, "Hi, I don't know what you're doing but I thought I could come down and we could have coffee. I can't believe it. You're my husband now."

*Pause.*

CARINA: Weird.

CHARLIE: I was thinking, Does she know she's talking to me?

*They walk.*

## 2 (continued)

JESSICA: Who were the people who could have saved us?

There was the artist who became a gentrifier. He went where few white people would go. He sought a different class as well. He stayed on after intimidation and burglary. He had romantic ideas about the landscape, while for those who lived there it was already a given: there didn't need to be another story told about it. So even though no one was asking for it, he made up a story, and built up around it. Before long, there was an audience of friends and family who wanted to support the artist. It had hope, not faked. It was an idyll made out of love, despite the poverty and abuse that surrounded it. There was even an understanding between the love on the inside and the love on the outside. It felt genuine, neighborly. Unbeknownst to him, he was paving the way for inevitable development by others with no relationship to what he thought was his community.

There was the activist who wanted her kids to go to a good school. The activist was a neighbor too, and she took on social justice causes, and fought for what her parents had instilled. Admirable and important work, she was distinct people because she actually did something meaningful toward change where most of us did not. When she fell in love and had kids, the concerns for humanity faded: who or what could supplant a parent's love for a child? Who could say no to what children desire? Besides, kids allowed the parent to think they were acting altruistically. And when it came to her schooling her children, a difficult choice had to be made: to send her kids to the local school or find something "better," more nurturing, more "well-rounded."

There was the philanthropist whose aesthetic was helplessly rooted in the landowning status quo. The foundation that was giving the money had a right not to give it, but they gave it away anyway. Even as the giving was based in certain aesthetic expectations. They gave the money out of love but somehow, it wasn't enough: it always was only one side of the equation.

But these types, flawed as they were, became the last bastion against crooks who only cared about themselves.

And those who slaved to have what we had: we built a monument on top of a pedestal to recognize what they did. Built it with a saying that captured how we felt about them and also how it represented their spirit. It stayed there in the square through snow and rain and sun. It stayed there, no one thought about it, even the families didn't think about it that much. Who was the message for, then, what did this erected thing need to speak to? Icon: eagle with spread wings; soldier advancing with rifle; a figure, Mary-like in her acceptance. Maybe it spoke to gods. The time got so old from now that the icons faded out and lost their shape and thereby their meaning. So old, that they wore away, eventually turning to dust. So old, it used to be: how lucky to be recognized by so many? Then those got forgotten, and replaced. Then the new ones disappeared from view, even quicker than the last. And the people who didn't forget, died, and on and on, until finally: "What's an icon?"

Take a look...I love this wall, our 600-year wall. The wall was to be built as protection from the natural world. And would that have been enough? Hardly. Myth was the wall that protected you. And you could have taken it down, you could have left it up. Instead, you moved on. To say we've moved on is to acknowledge, accept that we were our own demise. But how could we have been anything else!

I wish I could somehow play for you the songs—when even despite the drenching—what we came up with. We wanted to make something, still, real blues in open fourths and fifths, beautiful because: for whom was this?

# Scene 1

*Hospital. Children's ward. A shared room with two beds. Each room has a curtain on a track. From the next bed by the window, a family of four visits with the oldest daughter, fifteen years old, who is in the bed, recovering from back surgery.*

REVELATIONS: I don't wanna walk! Ow Owww Owie!!

DAD: Well, you have to walk. That's what the doctor, all these people want.

REVELATIONS: Don't want to, it hurts, Daddy.

DAD: I know, honey, but that's how you get better.

REVELATIONS: Ahhhhh! Ahh-ah! Owwieee! Can I sit down now?

DAD: No, that's not gonna help. *(to Mom)* Can you help me? *(to Revelations)* C'mon just one more lap. *(to Mom)* Hey, where you goin?

MOM: I'm gonna go smoke a cigarette. I did the last one. You can do this one.

REVELATIONS: Mommy!

MOM: What, I can't help you. Stop being a crybaby! You know what you have to do, she knows what she has to do.

DAD: Just a little further. Come on.

REVELATIONS: Why are you so crazy, Mom!

*The mom exits.*

OW OUCH OUCHIE!

DAD: Come on now. Keep a comin.

REVELATIONS: No no no no!! Shhhhs shshshhhhhh ssssss!

*They walk over to the bed.*

DAD: Ok, there you go. Now you get down. There's your reward.

REVELATIONS: Ahhhh...

DAD: Is that better?

REVELATIONS: Ahhh! Yes please don't make me do that again.

DAD: Well, I can't do that.

## Scene 2

*Hospital. Later. Revelations reaches for the IV pain killer.*

DAD: What are you doing?

REVELATIONS: Pushing the button.

*The mom and dad look at each other.*

DAD: All right.

*Revelations pushes the button.*

REVELATIONS: Where is my phone.

DAD: I am sure I don't know, Rev.

MOM: What do you need, hon?

REVELATIONS: I just want to play a game. I'm bored.

*Pause.*

MOM: ...Guys, I hate to say it but Walmart has good bread.

*Pause.*

The bird is in the garden.

REVELATIONS: What bird?

## Scene 3

*Hospital. Night. The parents are gathered around the bed. Revelations is reaching up into the space above her. She is asleep but her eyes are wide open.*

REVELATIONS: I want this...

DAD: Huh?

*She holds onto Dad's sleeve.*

REVELATIONS: No, I just...I can't get this off...

DAD *(to Mom)*: What is she doing?

*Revelations is holding outstretched arms, reaching past the dad, who leans over her.*

MOM: She's dreaming.

*Dad feels her head.*

DAD: She's burning up... *(shouting off)* Can we get a doctor in here?! *(to Mom)* I can't wake her up.

MOM: Just let her sleep.

DAD: You don't care?

MOM: Who says I don't care? How can you say that? That's what I'm asking.

DAD: There are two kinds of people: those who care and those who don't. And you can't change either. You can make endless excuses and justifications when you don't care.

MOM: Why are you saying all this. Do you mean me, specifically?

DAD: No, not necessarily.

MOM: Look. Sometimes, she is a crybaby, that's all.

REVELATIONS: Thanks, Mom.

MOM: You know you are. There's nothing wrong with that. You see, she is awake.

*Pause.*

And, ah...the people who don't care, can't change them either. They'll always find a reason not to care. Find a reason when she's well, then find a reason when she's sick and then. And then when she dies, find another reason to not care about that.

REVELATIONS: Mom! Why are you saying "she"?

MOM *(laughing)*: Don't take it personally.

REVELATIONS: Mom, I'm in the hospital. I'm so glad you can joke about my pain.

## Scene 4

*Hospital. Day. Mom is looking over some papers.*

MOM: Mmm...

DAD: What is it.

MOM: Our bill.

DAD: This place. Huhhhhh!! Why do we have insurance??

MOM: Well, it's a high deductible.

DAD: I swear to God, we're better off paying cash.

MOM: Well, it's not their fault.

DAD: Sure it is. Doctors. Insurance. Politicians. They can all go to hell.

REVELATIONS: Don't worry about it, Dad.

MOM: It's gonna work out.

DAD: Tired of these Indian lawyers and Jew doctors and government cocksuckers and chemicals in the sky, everywhere!...I'M SICK OF IT!

REVELATIONS: You'll get the money. You always figure out a way.

DAD: Well I'm out of ideas!

REVELATIONS: It's gonna be all right.

DAD: STOP SAYING THAT! HOW DO YOU KNOW. MAYBE IT'S NOT!!

REVELATIONS:

MOM: All right, that's enough. You're gonna wake up the little girl in the other bed.

*Pause.*

DAD *(crying)*: ...Just can't wait to see my girl up, being sarcastic and all. You have to get better.

*Pause.*

MOM: ...it feels kinda..._____ right now.

DAD: What do you mean?

REVELATIONS: Mom, stop being weird.

MOM: I'm not bein weird. You know what I mean. It feels kinda... propped up...and it...any moment...any moment...

REVELATIONS: Mom...

# 3

CHARLIE: Been thinkin 'bout you. Glad you could be here...My love is hard to describe, anyways I was hoping you could help me through my thinking...I want you to know why I don't go to church. Even though I'm baptized a Christian, and went to church off and on growing up, I don't really like being told how to worship or pray. Either that or I haven't found the right church for me. I do like the sense of community in most of the church services I've been to, especially in the Catholic church, which seems the most relaxed as far as decorum. But I want you to know that I do believe in you. And I pray every day to you. I started, though, only recently. And it's a trial kind of thing, I guess you could say. I spent many years not knowing what to believe, but I think part of it is I had to find my own path, and that's a cliché, but only until you find that path, because you will be surprised. Divine takes over fine and you give over, you reach up to the sky with nothing to lose in believing, so you believe with your heart and lose the sarcasm, the skepticism, drop the facade...I was surprised.

Ancients poured sacred bowls of unmixed wine, naked before the world's perils. They had sincere belief in their maker. What happened to their maker? I don't want a vengeful god, I'd rather have a benevolent compassionate one. I do believe in something bigger than me. That's what the worth is in what the ancients practiced. That there is something sacred in the universe. A sense of love and rightness. I can make my maker to my liking. If you're a believer you will receive that which you ask for. So I reached out to you because I was helpless. Everybody gets to that point and everybody has their own way of dealing with it. I could have died already and not known a path. I remember thinking when I felt helpless, and this was very recently, at night after I got into bed... "What do I have to lose?" It costs me nothing to pray. To ask the unknown or the unknowable and hope for a receiver. I think whether I go to church or not, I believe it has to be sincere. I want to tell you how beautiful you are with all the well-meaning I can muster. It's only through people that I love can I find any feelings for you. And places which I can't say I love but which inspired awe. I see three planes, or strata in space and your beauty pervades all three, from head to toe. Every inch, if I may, and what surrounds you is aglow. Featureless outline of a human form, perhaps also helpless in a way. Where else would you find compassion after all.

Lord
Let her live
Let her die
Of natural causes
My plea to God.

I will love you as best I can. Maybe your children are alive somewhere, and so this is to you. You've been absorbed into the daily minutia, no doubt, as I have, and unable to see most of the time what the stars at night show us. You're someone I haven't seen and may never see. Hardship and humiliation are as temporary as accomplishment, so I keep going. And I try to put up with people I don't like, especially when they are the loved ones of someone I love. As best I can I want to send you love and hope and pray that it finds you.

My grandparents never saw me mature. I know them mostly through stories. She was a teacher as best as I can tell and he taught Indians how to farm. We're more teachers than we know.

I can't imagine what you do, I hope you are healthy and happy as one can be, I hope you enjoy the light, I know I did. Please enjoy the light as it emerges each day.

Chances are you'll travel, so range. I want you to. Cross the high plains of each day. May you enjoy every day of it, and watch your children do the same.

# Allies (continued)

*Three travelers cross a desert. They roll up and down the hills.*

JESSICA: What's up, baby...You're quiet...You wish we could rise up and eat someplace, I know. Out of this place, well. There's no Applebee's out here—no Olive Garden, no sriracha sauce, no extra guac, no jumbo margarita...

ROBOT: Well, where is this restaurant? Where is this "rising up."

JESSICA: Aw, you don't get me. There was a time when you got me. I'm just sayin. We travel. We go on. Now we are in the desert. And. Where does it end?

ROBOT: I'm sure I don't understand. By "end" what do you mean?

JESSICA: Don't worry about it. Just know that you give me something, I give you something and that's how it's supposed to be.

ROBOT:

JESSICA: No help!

ROBOT:

JESSICA: I'm jokin around.

ROBOT:

JESSICA: You used to get me. But. You're a good friend. All things considered.

ROBOT: I am trying to help.

JESSICA: Save it. You're going to need the energy. I don't know how much battery you have left. I don't have another. It's just better all around if you let me do the talking. I don't mind. I got a lot to get off my chest. It helps to know you're listening. Just an ear, that's what I need right now...Anyways. Batteries are just all around in short supply, as you know...just wish there was somewhere a cache of batteries, you know what I'm saying?

*They come to a river.*

ROBOT: Look.

JESSICA: What?

ROBOT: *Look!*

JESSICA: Whoa wow...Wow!

ROBOT: How excited are we that we've come upon water?

JESSICA: Mm!

*Jessica drinks from the river.*

ROBOT:

JESSICA: What's wrong?

ROBOT: That's too deep to walk across.

JESSICA: What.

ROBOT: *I can't swim.*

JESSICA: Ok. *(to Elaine)* Can you swim?

*Elaine shakes her head.*

Get on my back.

*Elaine gets on Jessica's back.*

*(to the robot)* Come here, you too...What are you scared? Come on. You just hold onto her back and don't let go.

ROBOT: You can't swim.

JESSICA: Bro, I'm a lifeguard.

*Pause.*

No? Ok I'll take her across and then come back and get you.

*Jessica heads into the water with Elaine on her back until the water reaches her neck, then swims with Elaine holding on.*

You ok?

ELAINE:

*Jessica labors across capably using the breaststroke. Elaine clings tightly to her shoulders. Jessica finally finds the bottom of the other side and gets Elaine onto the shore, then turns to the robot.*

ROBOT: You were never coming back, were you.

JESSICA: I'm sorry.

ROBOT: I don wan to be the on who cares for all this stuff when the rest of you are gone.

JESSICA: What stuff??

*Pause.*

Don't worry. We'll come back.

ROBOT: To visit?

JESSICA: Maybe to live.

ROBOT: I don bel eve it.

JESSICA: Believe it or not. You don't want this to go to waste. Or to someone else. I understand that—it's important.

ELAINE: If it's so important then why don't you take care of it.

JESSICA: I can't. You know that part.

ROBOT: Well, no one can and it's not fair that I h ve to do it...it always comes to me to ta e care of this stuff and people take advantage of my concern...I like the plan y u stay here  n  g ard all this stuff.

JESSICA: I'm sure you do. No. I won't do it. Let it all rust. Or burn. Or break apart. I'm out.

ROBOT: An goo 0 ood bye?

JESSICA: What?

ROBOT: *G   ood bye*

*Jessica and Elaine laugh.*

JESSICA: What do you mean? "Gee-ood-bye?"

ROBOT: *I   m  e   a   g   od  b   y*

*The Evening* was co-commissioned by The Walker Art Center in Minneapolis and New York City Players. The Walker hosted its final production residency and presented the premiere on January 8–10, 2015. Directed by Richard Maxwell. Set and lights by Sascha van Riel. Costumes by Kaye Voyce. Dramaturgy by Molly Grogan. Original music by Richard Maxwell, arranged by the musicians.

Original Cast

Beatrice ——— Cammisa Buerhaus
Cosmo ——— Jim Fletcher
Asi ——— Brian Mendes

Band ——— James Moore, Andie Springer, David Zuckerman

*Samara* was produced by Soho Rep. and premiered in April 2017 at A.R.T./ New York Theatres. Directed by Sarah Benson, with original music and lyrics by Steve Earle. Set by Louisa Thompson. Costumes by Junghyun Georgia Lee. Lights by Matt Frey. Choreography by Annie-B Parson. Sound by Palmer Hefferan.

Original Cast

Narrator ——— Steve Earle
Messenger ——— Jasper Newell
Supervisor ——— Roy Faudree
Drunk ——— Paul Lazar
Manan ——— Becca Blackwell
Agnes ——— Vinie Burrows
Cowboy ——— Modesto Flako Jimenez
Beast ——— Matthew Korahais
Uilleann Pipes ——— Ivan Goff
Percussion ——— Anna Wray

*Paradiso* premiered in January 2018 at Greene Naftali in New York City. Produced by Greene Naftali and New York City Players. Directed by Richard Maxwell. Production design by Sascha van Riel. Costumes by Kaye Voyce. Technical Development by Zachary Davis and Scott Ponik.

Original Cast

Elaine Davis (Mom)
Jessica Gallucci
Carina Goebelbecker (Revelations)
Charlie Reina (Dad)

Richard Maxwell lives in New York City.